STOKE-ON-TRENT IN 50 BUILDINGS

MERVYN EDWARDS

AMBERLEY

Acknowledgements

The author would like to acknowledge Kenneth Edwards and family, Alan Mansell, Norman Scholes, *The Sentinel* newspaper, Gary Tudor, the Warrillow Collection at Keele University Library, and especially Ewart Morris.

Every effort has been made to correctly identify the copyright owners of the photographic materials used in this book. If, inadvertently, credits have not been correctly acknowledged, we apologise and promise to do so in reprinted editions.

First published 2018

Amberley Publishing, The Hill, Stroud
Gloucestershire gl5 4EP

www.amberley-books.com

Map contains Ordnance Survey data © Crown copyright and database right [2018]

British Library Cataloguing in Publication Data.
A catalogue record for this book is available from the British Library.

ISBN 978 1 4456 7781 1 (print)
ISBN 978 1 4456 7782 8 (ebook)

Origination by Amberley Publishing.
Printed in Great Britain.

Contents

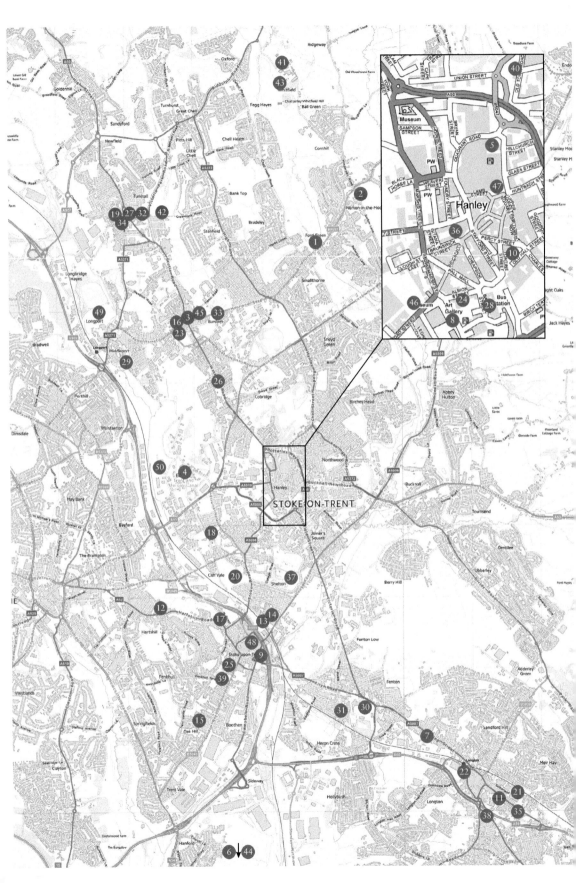

Key

1. Ford Green Hall, Ford Green Road, Smallthorne (1624)
2. St Bartholomew's Church, Norton Lane, Norton (1737/8)
3. The Big House, Moorland Road, Burslem (c. 1751)
4. Etruria Hall, Festival Way, Etruria (1771)
5. Former Church of St John the Evangelist, Town Road, Hanley (1790)
6. Mausoleum for the Marquis of Stafford, Stone Road, Trentham (1808)
7. Former Boundary Works, King Street, Longton (1819)
8. Bethesda Chapel, Albion Street, Hanley (1819)
9. St Peter ad Vincula Church, Church Street, Stoke (1830)
10. Former Covered Market, Tontine Square, Hanley (1831)
11. St James Church, Uttoxeter Road, Longton (1834)
12. Holy Trinity Church, Hartshill Road, Hartshill (1842)
13. Stoke Railway Station, Winton Square, Stoke (1848)
14. North Stafford Hotel, Winton Square, Stoke (1849)
15. The Villas, off London Road, Stoke (1851+)
16. Burslem Town Hall, Market Place (1857)
17. Roman Catholic Convent of Our Lady of the Angels and St Peter in Chains, Hartshill Road, Stoke (1857)
18. Etruscan Bone and Flint Mill (now the Etruria Industrial Museum; 1857)
19. Market Hall, Tunstall (1858)
20. Cemetery chapels, Cemetery Road, Hanley (1860)
21. Former Portland Works, Sutherland Road, Longton (1861)
22. Longton Town Hall, Times Square, Longton (1863)
23. Wedgwood Memorial Institute, Queen Street, Burslem (1869)
24. Hanley Town Hall, Albion Street, Hanley (1869)
25. Former Stoke Library, London Road, Stoke (1878)
26. No. 205 Waterloo Road, Cobridge (1880)
27. Tunstall Town Hall, High Street, Tunstall (1885)
28. Victoria Hall, Bagnall Street, Hanley (1888)
29. Middleport Pottery, Port Street, Middleport (1889)
30. Fenton Town Hall, Albert Square, Fenton (1889)
31. Christ Church, Christchurch Street, Fenton (1890)
32. Jubilee Buildings, the Boulevard, Tunstall (1889–91)
33. Former Miners' Hall, Moorland Road, Burslem (1893)
34. Clock Tower, Tower Square, Tunstall (1893)
35. Walkers' Nonsuch Ltd premises, Calverley Street, Longton (1894)
36. Former Bratt & Dyke shop, Trinity Street, Hanley (1896)
37. Pavilion, Hanley Park (1896)
38. Sutherland Institute, Lightwood Road, Longton (1899)
39. Former Falcon Works, Sturgess Street, Stoke (1902–05)
40. Golden Cup, Old Town Road, Hanley (c. 1912)
41. Lamphouse, former Chatterley Whitfield Colliery, Tunstall (1922)
42. The Roman Catholic Church of the Sacred Heart, Queen's Avenue, Tunstall (1930)
43. Pithead Baths and Canteen (now derelict), Chatterley Whitfield Colliery, near Tunstall (1938)
44. Wedgwood factory, Barlaston (1940)
45. Vale Park, Hamil Road, Burslem (1950)
46. Mitchell Memorial Youth and Arts Centre (now the Mitchell Arts Centre), Hanley (1957)
47. Potteries Shopping Centre (now Intu Potteries; 1988)
48. Civic Centre, Glebe Street, Stoke (1992)
49. Westport Lake Visitor Centre, near Tunstall (2009)
50. Vodafone Contact Centre, Etruria Valley Business Park (2009)

Introduction

There are fewer than 200 listed buildings within the boundaries of Stoke-on-Trent, with many of them deteriorating rapidly and several of them on English Heritage's Buildings At Risk register – telling us much about the city's struggle to hold onto its architectural treasures. Whether we blame the public or the private sector, it is a fact that handsome structures like the former Middleport rectory in Newcastle Street, Burslem, the King's Arms pub in Meir and Burslem's Municipal Cemetery chapel have all been demolished, while iconic town halls in Longton and Fenton have survived serious threats to their existence.

Some buildings are demolished because a new use cannot be found for them; conversion or reinvention is impracticable. Yet Stoke-on-Trent – acknowledged as a creative city – appears to be suffering from a malaise, a lack of imagination. No building is boarded up for very long without being condemned in the local press as an 'eyesore' with local people declaring, 'it wants knocking down!' It is this poverty of ideas that could have robbed Burslem of its most iconic building, as recounted in this book's section on the Town Hall.

Realists would always ask, how do you adapt a structure like Burslem Town Hall – assuming that those ace building converters, the JD Wetherspoon pub chain, haven't come in for it? Where there's a will, there's a way. Buildings elsewhere, rather than being knocked down to make way for shops, became shops. They include the Parade Shopping Centre in Shrewsbury (a former infirmary) and Dublin's classy Powerscourt Townhouse Centre, once a Georgian residence.

Sometimes, we spit on our past. The library in Burslem's Wedgwood Memorial Institute closed in 2011, afterwards standing derelict. Rewind to a meeting of dignitaries at Burslem Town Hall in January 1859, when James Edwards observed that 'he thought it would be a very poor compliment to Wedgwood to erect an institution which would afterwards fall into decay and disuse, and become a stigma to the neighbourhood'. Yet, in our brave new world of recent years, this is exactly what happened. There was even talk of demolishing the institute save for its marvellous tableau, but if you do this you ignore the original objective: not just to honour Josiah, but to encourage learning and craftsmanship. Now owned by the Prince's Regeneration Trust, the building stands every chance of reclaiming its place as a cultural centre in an increasingly creative, even bohemian town.

To conclude, how necessary is demolition and what sort of architectural legacy are we creating today? Stoke-on-Trent can learn much from other areas, and the Scarborough and District Civic Society is worth quoting here:

> Demolition is sometimes a fact of life but like a war it should be the very last resort, not the first. When we have to admit that a building has finally reached the end of its life then we should do our utmost to ensure that what replaces it is designed with sensitivity, and works in concert with its surroundings.

The 50 Buildings

1. Ford Green Hall, Ford Green Road, Smallthorne (1624)

Ford Green Hall was previously thought to have been erected between 1580 and 1600, but in 1991 experts in dendrochronology studied the annual growth rings of its timbers, coming up with the new date of 1624. The building is truly Stoke-on-Trent's great survivor.

Coal mining in the area can be traced back to medieval times. The earliest reference we have to the Ford family refers to a fatal accident in 1293, when 'Sibilla the widow of William de la Forde coming home from Newcastle [under Lyme] by the fields of Burwardeslyme [Burslem] fell into a pit of water from which coal had been dug and was drowned'. The Fords were leasing mines in the sixteenth century and became quite affluent on the profits.

The brick wing at north end of the hall was added in 1734.

Ford Green Hall, date unknown.

Ford Green Hall, date unknown.

It was originally known as Ford Green House, with that name being given in various sales particulars in the local press. It was only referred to as Ford Green Hall from the twentieth century.

The Fords of Ford Green House were yeoman farmers and the value of the land they farmed is indicated in the family's wills and inventories, many of which have been transcribed by Nigel Coulton. When the house was up for sale in 1802 there were around 60 acres of 'excellent Arable, Meadow and Pasture Land' attached.

The Fords owned the property until c. 1790, after which its fortunes declined. It was converted into three or four workers' cottages in the nineteenth century, and was purchased by the council in 1946. The council painted the exterior wooden beams black to give it what we refer to as the 'magpie house' look – favoured by the Victorians who often painted exposed timbers with black bitumen and applied whitewashed plaster to the wattle and daub infill. In more recent years, the paint has been removed, and rightly so.

The property has sunk through subsidence from coal mining – a process begun by the Fords themselves. The council opened the house as a folk museum in 1952. It survived horrendous flooding in 1987 and continues to operate as a tourist attraction.

2. St Bartholomew's Church, Norton Lane, Norton (1737/8)

Visitors to this elevated site are guaranteed a fabulous view over the moors and fine air quality.

In 1737, this Anglican church – which had a spire, as shown on one surviving illustration – was adjudged to be 'in a very decayed and ruinous condition'. It was taken down on 3 May.

Above and below: St Bartholomew's Church, 2014 and 1995.

The foundations of the new church were marked out on 6 May and it was built by Richard Trubshaw. By 1775, it was 'a plain small edifice of brick ... a square tower at the west end has its top corners ornamented with 4 balls or small globes, and is remarkable for containing the only doors of entrance, the chief of which is on the west side, and leads into the body of the church'.

Norton-in-the-Moors, previously dependent upon St Peter's in Stoke, became a separate parish in 1807. The church was extended in 1914 by architect J. H. Beckett. According to the *Staffordshire Advertiser*, he preserved 'the severe classical style of the original, but by a judicious use of arches, he has produced an interior which in its simple dignity is extremely effective'. The improvements were dedicated in October and included the eastern portion of the nave, with transepts, the chancel sanctuary, organ chambers and vestries.

3. The Big House, Moorland Road, Burslem (c. 1751)

This building needs to be described in relation to the factory that once stood behind it. The Big House Works was built in a location where brothers Thomas and John Wedgwood – the owners of the Red Lion estate – could harness the elements. They had a good supply of water and, with the site being on an elevation, at the Jenkins they also built a windmill for flint-grinding purposes. The architect was James Brindley, who had recently set up as a millwright in Burslem.

The Big House is the earliest surviving example of a manufacturer's house. It was built for the brothers Thomas and John, the kinsmen of the great Josiah Wedgwood (1730–95)

The Big House, 1994.

The Big House, date unknown.

and designed in the Palladian style. It is a symmetrical five-bay, three-storey building with a projecting middle bay and a pediment topping the whole. The window lintels are of rusticated stone while the central windows are given emphasis by stone architraves. There is a pedimented porch incorporating Tuscan columns.

When first built, its size and dignity would have conspicuously advertised the status of the Wedgwood brothers and the key role they were playing as the Industrial Revolution unfolded in Burslem. The brothers retired in 1763. Thomas Wedgwood died childless in 1776 and John in 1780.

In his *History of the Potteries* (1829), Simeon Shaw wrote that the scale and style of the property far excelled all other dwellings in the district, hence the name of the Big House.

The property was famously the Midland Bank for half a century, and in 1879, a sandstone wall was demolished to the rear. Workmen discovered several cavities in the wall, inside of which was a large amount of old pottery that had been secreted by master potter and antiquarian Enoch Wood in 1810. The wall had been built by Thomas Wedgwood.

The Big House stands today as a reminder of two of the most successful capitalists the town has ever known. It is Grade II* listed. At one time there was a walled forecourt and entrance gates, but these were removed in 1956. Today, the house looks rather hemmed in by two extremely busy roads.

4. Etruria Hall, Festival Way, Etruria (1771)

The home of Josiah Wedgwood (1730–95) was designed by Derby architect Joseph Pickford and built between 1768 and 1771, a little to the north-east of Josiah's new factory of

Above: Etruria Hall, date unknown.

Below: Etruria Hall, view from Festival Way, 2012.

1769. The house was erected on the 350-acre Ridge House estate, purchased in December 1767 from the son of Mrs Ashenhurst, with whom Josiah had been embroiled in much time-consuming negotiation.

Historian Ernest Warrillow recorded that Wedgwood's family took up residence at the hall on 11 November 1769. Later that day, a large number of his workpeople were entertained at Burslem Town Hall by way of celebration. The residence overlooked a gentleman's park, designed by notable landscape gardener William Eames. The ornamental grounds embraced a Chinese bridge, a summer house, fishponds and nurseries, giving some idea of how Wedgwood saw his social status by this time. On the one hand, he required a handsome house and gardens for his family and the guests he wished to entertain, such as George Stubbs, Joseph Priestly, Erasmus Darwin, James Watt and Sir William Hamilton. On the other hand, the house reflected the restless mind of a busy master potter. Its vaulted cellars contained Josiah's private laboratories where he conducted experiments on colours and glazes.

An early depiction of Etruria Hall was painted with enamel colours on a plaque, *c.* 1773. It shows the Trent and Mersey Canal in the foreground and the hall without wings. Two wings were added to Etruria Hall in 1780, offering more room for Wedgwood's growing family as well as accommodation for Alexander Chisholm, Wedgwood's secretary, assistant and chemist. Other additions included a school room, billiard room and drawing room.

Internally, Etruria Hall could boast of friezes, cornices and ceiling paintings designed by John Flaxman Jr. Meteyard described the main rooms in the 1860s, but very little of the original hall has survived. The cellars are the least altered feature of the house.

Etruria Hall has had a variegated history since the departure of the Wedgwood family and is now a conference centre linked by a covered walkway to the Moat House Hotel, which opened in 1991.

5. Former Church of St John the Evangelist, Town Road, Hanley (1790)

Hanley's principal Anglican church was built in 1737/8 and replaced by the present building of 1790. There were alterations from 1870, when it was considered that the architecture and fittings of St John's were looking outdated. A major addition at this stage was the Gothic-style chancel of 1871. The architect was W. Palmer, and the builder, Mr Matthews.

Bear in mind that Gothic was back in favour by this stage. Contemporary taste was influencing the design of churches. The *Staffordshire Weekly Times* reported in 1871:

> St John's church is a building of the last century, when ecclesiastical architecture was at its lowest depth, and its ugly square of bricks was no doubt at that day not considered deficient in beauty, and even so recent an author as Ward, the historian, speaks of it as a 'stately pile'. Churches are looked upon with different eyes to-day, and the Old Church could not be expected to escape from the commendable appetite for church improvement which has of late prevailed.

This opinion encapsulated the rather typical Victorian view of Georgian architecture. We are reminded that the design of William Smith's St Giles (Newcastle) of 1721 was criticised by Sir George Gilbert Scott in the 1870s, before being rebuilt by him.

Above and below: Former St John's Church, 1998 amd 2012.

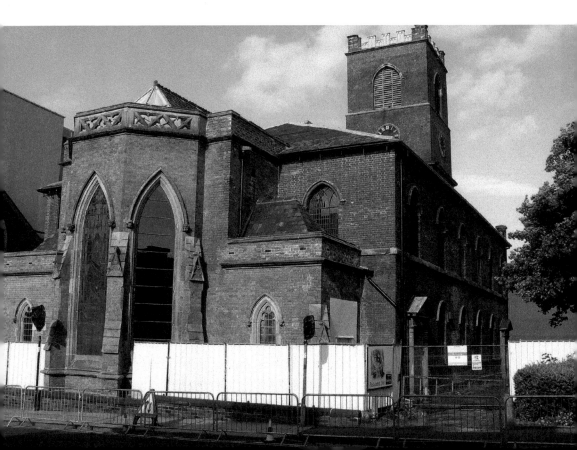

The whole structure was restored in 1885. The brickwork was renovated, and the old stone pinnacles on the tower were supplanted by cast-iron ones. In 1986 a devastating fire caused £50,000 worth of damage to the rapidly deteriorating structure, and rendered the church virtually unusable. However, it remained a protected building – listed, Grade II* – on account of its Gothic-style red-brick west tower of 1790 and its cast-iron features (including the columns that support the gallery). It is one of the world's earliest surviving examples of the architectural use of cast iron.

It was not a listed building that remained intact. The tower battlements were removed for safety reasons in 2003. Described by *Sentinel* columnist Dave Proudlove as 'a monument to the apathy and neglect of the city's built heritage', the building reopened as the Six Towns Antiques and Vintage Emporium in 2017.

6. Mausoleum for the Marquis of Stafford, Stone Road, Trentham (1808)

The only Grade I-listed building in Stoke-on-Trent stands in its own grounds opposite the main gates to Trentham Gardens. It was designed by Charles Heathcote Tatham of Trentham and erected for the Marquis of Stafford, later the Duke of Sutherland. It was the last resting place for members of the Sutherland family of Trentham Hall.

Mausoleum, 2017.

Mausoleum, 2017.

In May 1808, the *Staffordshire Advertiser* reported that it was 'a building of singular construction, being the only edifice of the sort in the country'. Internally, the stone-built structure contained forty catacombs under one groined arch of stone. The whole was lined with beautifully dark and highly polished marble. White's Directory (1834) recorded that only one of the catacombs was occupied by that time, 'the remains of the daughter of the present Duke'.

This mighty neo-Egyptian structure is a grim, and according to Pevsner 'isolated' building, but in July 2017 it was announced by Stoke-on-Trent City Council that overgrown mature yew trees were to be cut back in order to open up the view of the mausoleum. It is owned by the diocese of Lichfield but the lack of funds available for its upkeep have seen the mausoleum placed on Historic England's At Risk register.

7. Former Boundary Works, King Street, Longton (1819)

Here's a rambling old potworks that offers a whiff of bygone Longton, displaying a magnificent frontage of symmetry, grace and style. From the outset, it was meant to impress visitors and those travelling along the arterial road through Longton. The central projecting bay encompassed an archway entrance with keystones. Above it was a Venetian window, similar to many that adorned Potteries buildings, including Mason's Ironstone Works in Hanley, the Greenfields Pottery in Tunstall and the positively exquisite Hill Pottery in Westport

Above and right: Former Boundary Works, 2015.

Road, Burslem – all now demolished. Also in evidence on the central bay is a Diocletian window similar to that which adorned Wedgwood's Etruria Works. We also note the brick dentilling beneath the eaves across the entire length of the frontage, and a date stone (1819).

Like similarly large pot-banks, the seventeen-bay Boundary (or California) Works advertised, through its dignity and beauty, the respectability of the owner – Jacob Marsh, who built it. However, the stateliness of exteriors was never a guarantee of exemplary standards behind, as we learn from such accounts as that of potter Charles Shaw, who observed unspeakable conditions in the workshops of the Hill Pottery in Burslem in the 1840s.

The Boundary Works was Grade II listed in 1972.

8. Bethesda Chapel, Albion Street, Hanley (1819)

Both beautiful and dignified, the Bethesda Chapel building nevertheless offers a story embracing religious and political fermentation that was to embroil some of the most powerful figures in the growing town of Hanley.

To many of its devotees, Methodism had become top-heavy and autocratic in its direction by the 1790s. The all-powerful Methodist Conference was seen by many as a hidebound controlling axis that was squeezing the life out of a religion that had once spoken from the heart. With the death of founder John Wesley in 1791, tensions became more transparent and many Methodists pushed for greater democracy in the movement. Convinced that their demands were being ignored, many seceded from the main Wesleyan body and in 1797 the Methodist New Connexion was formed under the leadership of Revd Alexander Kilham.

Bethesda Chapel, 1999.

Bethesda Chapel, 2012.

He and other dissidents met in a private house and then a coach house in Albion Street before building a chapel capable of accommodating 600 worshippers in 1798.

With Hanley as the head of the circuit, the popularity of the movement soon necessitated the expansion of the chapel (1811) prior to the erection of a new place of worship in 1819. It was designed by J. H. Perkins, who was a schoolmaster by profession, not an architect. Described as being 'one of the largest outside of the Metropolis', it was opened in May 1820. It could accommodate 3,000 worshippers if space in the aisles was used.

Many improvements were made over the years, including, most notably, the refronting of the chapel in 1859 by Robert Scrivener. Hanley's political, commercial and social elite worshipped at Bethesda, including the Ridgway family, Joseph Clementson, Michael Huntbach, Oliver Dyke and James Dudson.

The chapel closed in 1985 and since then has known many vicissitudes. It has been owned by the Historic Chapels Trust since 2002, and following its appearance on the hit TV series *Restoration!* in 2003 has undergone splendid renovation and repair. It is a Grade II*-listed building whose Italianate frontage incorporates an octastyle portico supported by eight Corinthian columns and a Venetian window. The interior is equally magnificent.

9. St Peter ad Vincula Church, Church Street, Stoke (1830)

St Peter's in Stoke – now Stoke Minster – is the ecclesiastical hub of the Potteries. It served a huge parish and was an ancient place of worship. Stoke was 'The Place of the Church'.

The new church was built to the north of its medieval predecessor between 1826 and 1829 to the designs of Trubshaw and Johnson. It could boast a large five-bay nave and a 112-foot tower surmounted by a parapet of battlements and pinnacles. Numerous manufacturers occupied their own pews, including Herbert Minton, who was a churchwarden there. It was consecrated in 1830.

St Peter's Church, 1996.

St Peter's Church, 2013.

It's important to point out that St Peter's is a minster, not a cathedral. The city of Stoke is not a diocese and therefore doesn't have a cathedral. However, there were plans to enhance its status back in the 1920s.

The historian John Ward had described the 1830 church as an 'elegant modern edifice ... [built] in a superior style of architectural beauty'. That may well have been the contemporary view, but it wasn't to last. By the 1920s, many people felt that St Peter's was not worthy of the title of the Mother Church of the Potteries, and in July 1926 Sir Giles Gilbert Scott was asked for his opinion. He answered: 'It hardly needs any special knowledge of architecture to realize that the church is an extremely bad example of the Gothic style.' He wasn't the first to criticise the clumsy Gothic style of the 1830s/40s – see our entry for St James (Longton).

So Scott urged the demolition of St Peter's and the erection of a totally new church, reflecting its importance in Stoke-on-Trent, which was granted city status in 1925. Scott was asked to draw up plans for the new edifice. They appeared in *The Sentinel* newspaper and bear a strong similarity to Liverpool Cathedral, which of course, he designed. The plan was to lay the foundation stone of the new church to mark the centenary of the present church's consecration. However, despite the many meetings, it was never built. At an estimated cost of £150,000, it was eventually considered too expensive a project to proceed with.

10. Former Covered Market, Tontine Square, Hanley (1831)

This former covered market – built as a specialist butchers' market and designed by Joseph Turner – stands near to Market Square and reminds us of Hanley's early commercial might.

A body of trustees was established in 1791 and granted statutory authority by Act of Parliament in 1813. This Act also sanctioned Hanley's market. The trustees were empowered to improve the marketplace, with the result that an old market house was taken down and a poultry and butter market built in 1819 in what is now Fountain Square. A body of Improvement Commissioners who supervised policing and lighting was set up in 1825, with the power to appoint a chief bailiff, constables and watchmen.

From the 1830s onwards, Market Square was improved significantly, with lasting benefits for muscle-flexing Hanley. Market Square became the retail hub of the Potteries, and in 1831, the covered butchers' market – or the shambles – was unveiled as part of Hanley's new vision.

The market trustees built the butchers' market – an enormous classical building designed in the Grecian Doric style. It could accommodate 122 butcher's stalls. It incorporated a spacious yard, offices and a weighing machine. Internally, it was lit with seventy bat-wing gaslights.

One correspondent wrote to the local press in early 1832 about the condition of some of the meat offered for sale. Some of the butchers were alleged to have been in the habit of procuring cattle at a cheap rate, no matter how unfit for killing and selling. Some of this

Meat Market, 1970s.

The Reginald Mitchell pub, 2014.

meat was only sold in the building in the evenings, so that its dubious condition was less visible to potential buyers.

Like so many public buildings of this time, the covered market effectively became multipurpose. In 1832, the passing of the Great Reform Bill – prematurely seen as a great reason for celebration by artisans – was marked with a dinner for between 2,000 and 3,000 working persons at the covered market, where a large quantity of beef was foremost on the menu – hopefully of good quality!

The market building closed in 1987 and now accommodates the Reginald Mitchell (Wetherspoon's) pub and Waterstones bookshop.

11. St James Church, Uttoxeter Road, Longton (1834)

St James' Church was consecrated on the same day as St Mark's in Shelton, and this is not the only connection between them. Their architecture is very similar, though the *North Staffordshire Mercury* recorded that the Longton church was, by comparison, 'in some respects plainer in its external appearance, particularly about the tower'. Nevertheless, historian John Ward described it as a very good specimen of plain Gothic architecture of the Perpendicular style. It was built by Trubshaw and Johnson.

St James' Church, date unknown.

St James' boasted massive circular turrets at its angles and incorporated pinnacles and battlements, its tower being built to a height of 90 feet. The chancel has a five-sided east end.

Constructed from Hollington stone, St James' could seat 2,000 worshippers, offering far more accommodation than was ever required. For the reasons why, we must consider the zeitgeist that precipitated the vigorous flourishing of Anglican church buildings at this period.

St James' belongs to that class of ecclesiastical buildings known as Commissioners' or Waterloo churches. This huge church dominated a grimy, heavily polluted, industrial area of the town. Some of the worst Longton slums were located around St James', while the Garfield Works manufactory and the Three Cups beerhouse directly opposite contrasted sharply with the resplendent church in its 2-acre grounds.

In 1818 an Act provided £1 million for the building of Anglican churches in developing urban areas. A second £0.5 million was offered in 1825. This was both a reaction to the increasing number of dissenting chapels and an attempt to reassert social control through religion at a time when radical political movements were gaining ground at home, and when the English Establishment – as expressed by the graphic cartoons of James Gillray – was terrified that bloody revolution might occur in England as it had in France.

The architectural style of many of the Commissioners' churches led to them being arraigned as Gothic hotchpotches, lacking in historical authenticity. Other Commissioners' churches included Christ Church in Tunstall and St Paul's in Dale Hall (demolished in 1974).

Holy Trinity Church in Hartshill was an attempt to reassert true Gothic, as we shall see.

St James' Church, 2015.

12. Holy Trinity Church, Hartshill Road, Hartshill (1842)

Holy Trinity Church was founded by Herbert Minton and intended to cater for the spiritual needs of a village whose population had grown to approximately 1,000 residents by 1840.

The architect was the young George Gilbert Scott (1811–78), who was largely responsible for the mid-nineteenth-century Gothic Revival in England, though he confessed his indebtedness to Pugin, whose St Giles Church (1841–46) – Pugin's Gem – is located in Cheadle. The common link between both churches is that both are adorned by Herbert Minton's tiles. Indeed, Scott, Pugin and Minton formed a triangle of creativity, as Minton made the floor tiles – designed by Pugin – that adorned the floors of the Houses of Parliament. Pugin wrote to Minton and declared that they were the best tiles in the world and that 'my patterns and your workmanship go ahead of anything'. They remained friends until Pugin died in 1852. In many respects, Minton and Pugin were both pushing in the same direction. Minton revived the production of encaustic floor tiles and adapted medieval tile-making techniques, while Pugin himself believed that the Gothic architecture of medieval times most represented the high ideals of what you might call the golden age of the Christian church. Minton and Pugin, therefore, was a business partnership made in heaven.

Left and below: Holy Trinity Church, 1996 and 2016.

Both Pugin and Scott were responsible for transforming the architectural style dubbed 'Commissioners' Gothic' into a more well-rounded, authentic Gothic. St James the Less in Longton is only eight years older than Holy Trinity, but the difference between the two is stark. Pevsner describes Holy Trinity as 'entirely Camdenian, or rather Puginian, i.e. it appears with the claim to be genuine Middle Pointed'. The church more closely resembles St Giles' Catholic Church in Cheadle than it does St James.

In 1862, the original square chancel was taken down and replaced by a new apsidal chancel funded by Colin Minton Campbell in memory of his uncle, Herbert Minton (died 1858). The walls were lined with Minton encaustic tiles and the builder was Mr Evans of Ellastone, the entire cost being around £2,000. The architect was again Scott.

13. Stoke Railway Station, Winton Square, Stoke (1848)

Winton Square was famously described by Nikolaus Pevsner as 'the finest piece of Victorian axial planning in the county' and surely shows Stoke at its most stately.

Stoke railway station was constructed for the North Staffordshire Railway and accommodated the company's boardroom and main offices. The station consolidated Stoke-upon-Trent's status as the communications capital of the Potteries.

The architect credited by the *Staffordshire Advertiser* at the time of its opening was H. A. Hunt of London, who also receives the credit from Pevsner. However, other sources attest that he only assisted the otherwise unknown architect, R. A. Stent. The contractor was Mr Jay, of London Wall.

Stoke railway station, 2002.

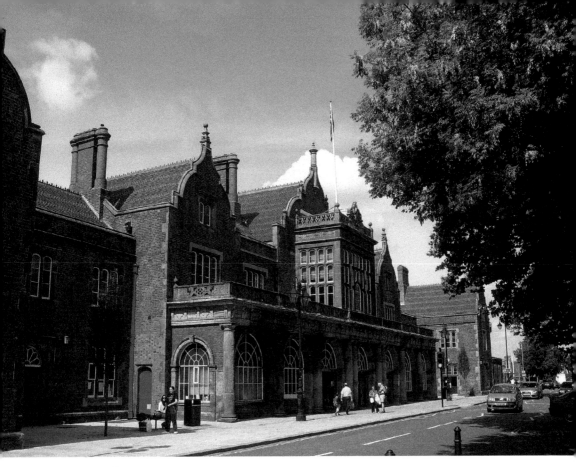

Stoke railway station, 2013.

The station and adjacent buildings are Elizabethan to Jacobean in style. It was designed with gabled parapets, mullioned and transomed windows and 'old fashioned brick chimneys'. We also note the local red brick, broken up with blue-brick diapering, and prominent Dutch-style gables.

It's well known that there was sex segregation in many Victorian buildings, including schools and workhouses, but it's interesting to note that Stoke station was built with waiting rooms for ladies and gentlemen.

The Knotty directors' board room was immediately above the central doorway.

Charles Knight, writing in the late 1840s, described the 'Tudor' architecture and recorded that 'the whole of the appointments have a completeness and a high finish which we are accustomed to look for only at the great terminal stations of the railways'. He also praised the tessellated pavements, laid under the corridors of the two fronts of the station, as being designed by Messrs Minton's in Stoke. Alterations followed over the years, notably in 1870, when the seven-arch stone portico was glazed in.

Other railway stations on the line were designed in a similar Jacobean style, perhaps notably that at Stone. The original Stone railway station of 1848 was replaced by the present one in 1849. Another railway station that incorporates a few similar ideas is to be found at Shrewsbury. T. M. Penson's 1848 masterpiece is described as having a 'mildly Tudor character' also including mullioned windows and tall chimneys. Stoke railway station was listed Grade II* in 1972.

14. North Stafford Hotel, Winton Square, Stoke (1849)

This building was one of three hotels ultimately owned by the North Staffordshire Railway, the others being the Rudyard Hotel and the Churnet Valley Hotel (built originally as a house). Upon opening, the North Stafford incorporated four storeys and was designed in the style of a Jacobean manor house.

Charles Knight described what is now the North Stafford Hotel as follows:

> A railway-hotel lies eastward of the station, which must take rank among the most elegant things of the kind in the kingdom. It is built precisely in harmony with the station itself; and with its stables and out-houses, has the appearance of an old English mansion of the larger kind – so far at least as that can appear old which is newly from the workman's hands.

The Railway Hotel served the North Staffordshire Railway very favourably – in May 1898 a dinner was held there for twenty-nine men who had joined the company in its earliest years (1846–48).

In assessing the importance of this building, we must look beyond its magnificent architecture, for the hotel swiftly became the foremost venue for meetings and social events in the area, effectively superseding the revered Swan Hotel in Hanley, which had been a high-profile rendezvous point for businessmen and others until its closure and demolition in the 1840s. On occasions, food was prepared at the hotel and served across the road in the boardroom of the railway station.

North Stafford Hotel, 1994.

North Stafford Hotel, 2013.

The hotel appeared in Arnold Bennett's novels as the Five Towns Hotel. In Arnold Bennett's short story, *The Dog*, he described the hotel as 'the greatest hotel in North Staffordshire. It has two hundred rooms. It would not entirely disgrace Northumberland Avenue. In the Five Towns it is august, imposing and unique'.

The modern entrance canopy serves an important purpose, especially for hotel visitors waiting for taxis, though detracting from the splendour of the building itself.

Other examples of the so-called Jacobethan style of architecture include the former Savings Bank in Welsh Row, Nantwich, and further afield, Scarborough Town Hall, built as a private house in 1852 and extended in the same style in 1901.

15. The Villas, off London Road, Stoke (1851+)

The finest middle-class housing in Stoke-on-Trent was erected between 1851 and 1885 off London Road in Stoke by Stokeville Building Society. Private enterprise produced an innovative scheme wherein the society's members were to build and own properties on copyhold land that would be known as Stokeville. At first, many of the owners chose not to live in the new properties, letting them out to tenants instead. Leading architect Charles Lynam – who was appointed through the influence of Herbert Minton as the society's architect – designed three classes of house (first, second and third), his Italianate villa style

The Villas, 2018.

proving a real eye-catcher. We note the widespread use of stucco over brick, overhanging eaves and tiles roofs.

It is interesting to consider the influences of Lynam, who was only twenty-one when the building society was formed. The Historic Buildings Survey commissioned by Stoke-on-Trent City Council in 1984 remarked:

> Charles Lynam owed a great debt with his designs to a much earlier nineteenth century tendency in residential building which took the Italianate Villa – via the paintings of Claude and Poussin – as its model. However, whereas this earlier interest in villas had been characterised as a means of providing a 'modest retreat for gentlemen', it had by the 1840s also become one to which the suburban middle classes also aspired. This would indicate that Charles Lynam's designs were a very late contribution to an architectural fashion already in decline.

His twenty-four superior houses offered seclusion from the main road, with each being attached to a smart plot of land suitable for development as gardens. The properties provided 'live-in' accommodation for servants.

The Villas, 2018.

Among the notable figures who lived at the Villas were Joseph F. L. Arnoux, a pottery designer at Minton's (died 1902), fellow Minton designer Louis Marc Solon (died 1913) and Arnold Machin, who designed the portrait of Elizabeth II that has appeared on postage stamps since 1967 (died 1999).

The Villas are notable for having been designated Stoke's first Conservation Area, although in more recent times some have been subdivided into apartments.

16. Burslem Town Hall, Market Place (now the Haywood Academy Sixth Form Centre; 1857)

Burslem's second town hall of 1857 replaced a predecessor of 1761. Constructed from millstone grit, it had a rusticated exterior to the ground floor that incorporated large windows with deeply coved jambs and arches. Above were coupled pilasters of the Corinthian order and wide, arched windows that illuminated the interior.

At the west end was a portico with a rusticated basement and an arched entrance sufficiently wide to allow carriages to drive to the doors and for their passengers to alight under cover.

The façade incorporated an elegant clock turret, with four faces, supported by eight caryatids. Caryatids are female figures that support an entablature in classical architecture.

It has been noted that there was a great geometrical or mathematical precision about classical architecture, with pilasters and figures such as caryatids used to pace out the dimensions of a building. However florid Burslem's town hall may seem to us, its dimensions do conform fairly closely to rule-bound classical architecture. However, the building is also a reminder of how contemporary artists copied bygone styles according to the dictates of new ideas and fashions. Many town halls and other public buildings that were erected around the country were often bastard Roman, Greek or even Egyptian in design.

Topping the whole was a winged figure of Civic Victory. The figure blends two ideas: Victoria, the Roman goddess of victory, and the civic crown. Elsewhere, we find similar ideas. Berlin has the Siegessaule Victory Column, inaugurated in 1873. It is topped by the bronze statue of Victoria, designed by Freidrich Drake. Berliners have given the statue the nickname Goldelse, meaning something like 'Golden Lizzy'. Burslem people call their similar figure the Golden Angel.

In 1969, some newspaper correspondents suggested that the town hall should be demolished in favour of more shopping facilities. One *Sentinel* reader described the town hall as a monstrosity. Even some councillors wished to demolish it and replace it with a modern shopping precinct.

Following periods as Burslem Leisure Centre and the Ceramica exhibition hall, the Grade II*-listed building became the Haywood Academy Sixth Form Centre.

Former Burslem Town Hall, 1994.

17. Roman Catholic Convent of Our Lady of the Angels and St Peter in Chains, Hartshill Road, Stoke (1857)

It is fascinating how architecture of a certain vintage is now viewed by people in the light of their own cultural references. To the untrained eye swayed by twentieth-century film-makers, a Gothic-style house will always be 'spooky'. Likewise, Richard Weir in his book *Six of the Best* (1986) described this building as 'like some latter-day Colditz'.

Originally built to accommodate the Sisters of Penance of the 3rd Order of St Dominic, who were affiliated to the Convent at Stone, this straggling building was opened as a work in progress in 1857 with a new chancel by A. E. Purdie added in 1884–85.

Designed by Charles Hansom, it is in the Gothic style of 1300 and described by Pevsner as 'wholly informal'. It is worth noting that the Medieval Court at the Great Exhibition of 1851 had helped to take the popularity of the Gothic style to a new level.

Externally, this edifice was built with red and yellow bricks in separate bands, with the lighter colour allowed to dominate. There were five courses of yellow or buff-coloured bricks to two of red, while Hollington stone dressings are also used.

The baptistry was almost inevitably floored with Minton encaustic tiles.

Roman Catholic Convent of Our Lady of the Angels and St Peter in Chains, 1995.

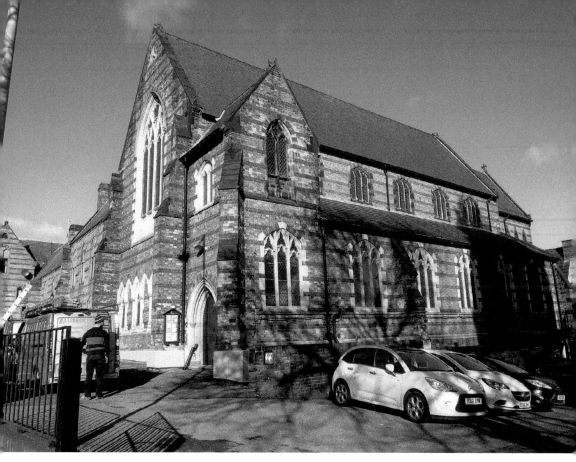

Roman Catholic Convent of Our Lady of the Angels and St Peter in Chains, 2018.

18. Etruscan Bone and Flint Mill (now the Etruria Industrial Museum; 1857)

With the expansion of the ceramic industry in the nineteenth century, there was an increase in ancillary trades. Grinding mills became more abundant. Some of these were owned by manufacturers and erected on their premises – such as at Wedgwood's – while others were owned and run independently. The Furlong Mill in Burslem (1843) and the Etruscan Bone and Flint Mill at Etruria were such operations.

Here, materials were ground for the agricultural and pottery industries. Bourne and Hudson were operating such a business in Etruria by 1820 according to a bill head of July 1857 – the date being repeated on numerous advertisements from this point onwards.

Jesse Shirley & Son took over the business and built a new mill on-site in 1857, constructed by George Kirk of Etruria, who was a leading builder who specialised in mills. It stood at the junction of the Trent and Mersey and Caldon canals.

The christening of the mill was not celebrated until 31 December 1859, when Jesse and sixty of his friends and workmen ate a substantial dinner at the Etruria Inn. The mill survives today, its frontage bearing the date of 1857. Jesse Shirley had two sons who were later to take over the works: Jesse Jr (1848–1927) and Henry Benjamin Shirley (1858–1910).

In later years, the Etruscan Bone and Flint Mill became affected by subsidence. Shirley's mill ceased production in 1972, having used virtually the same process and machinery up until this time. By this stage, the subsidence-affected building had decayed and it

Above: Industrial Museum, 2016.

THE FLINT KILN

Left: Danielle Evans, visitor guide at the Etruria Industrial Museum, 2017.

was difficult to modernise it. It was the last steam-driven mill in Britain and the site was scheduled as an Ancient Monument in 1975. The mill was later restored by volunteers and was officially reopened on 6 April 1991 by TV personality and steeplejack Fred Dibnah. The sterling work of volunteers continues to underpin the success of the museum and visitor centre. A particular attraction is the beam engine *Princess*, reputed to have been made by the company of Bateman & Sherratt of Salford in around 1820. It was installed on-site in 1856.

19. Market Hall, Tunstall (1858)

The market history of Tunstall properly begins in 1816 with the laying out of a marketplace – now Tower Square. However, the new Market Hall was one of the initiatives of the Board of Health, which opened on 2 December 1858.

It was erected on the east side of the square, directly overlooking High Street, as can be seen on the 1878 Ordnance Survey map. Standing on 0.5 acres of land, it was built of brick enclosures with stone facings and had a roof divided into five spans, as well as side roofs. Inside the main entrance were lodges for the accommodation of the hall keeper, the inspector of weights and measures and the collector of tolls. The floor was paved with York

Covered market, 2018.

Tony Stanfield premises in the covered market, 2017.

flagging. The architect of the building was G. T. Robinson, who also designed Burslem Town Hall.

At the opening, one speaker, E. Wedgwood, suggested that though the building appeared more spacious than required the time might arrive when it was too small, as he hoped that Tunstall would one day become 'the metropolis of the Potteries'. The hall should thus be seen as proof of Tunstall's aspirations. However, size proved not to be everything. By the early 1880s, it was not only considered to be too large but had become structurally faulty on account of subsidence.

Part of the site was assigned for the new Town Hall (1883–85), with the remaining part of the old building still housing Tunstall's indoor market. It boasts single-storey arcaded fronts with heavily rusticated round-headed entrances both from the Boulevard and Butterfield Place.

By 1992, the covered market had dangerous structural weaknesses, including buckled trusses and weakened cast-iron supporting columns. The repair work was due to begin in 1994, and fifty-five stallholders were transferred to a temporary building in Woodland Street. However, shortage of funds led to the renovation being delayed. Heritage Lottery Fund money was secured for the project in 1998 and it ultimately reopened at the beginning of the twenty-first century. The Market Hall, in part a relic of the mid-nineteenth century, remains a very valuable town amenity, offering an old-fashioned but thoroughly enjoyable shopping experience.

2c. Cemetery chapels, Cemetery Road, Hanley (1860)

Stoke-on-Trent's first municipal cemetery was consecrated in Hanley in 1860 with these beautiful chapels as an attractive centrepiece. The elegance of the design – by Henry Ward & Son – demands our attention, though to some observers it constituted something of an architectural mish-mash. The *Staffordshire Advertiser*, magisterially declaring itself as a devout admirer of 'pure Gothic', reported:

> Generally speaking, the style of the chapels may be considered as transitional from the Early English to the Decorated Gothic; but the numerous gables and the curiously truncated roofs show that the severe English Gothic has been modified by the introduction of a foreign element doubtless with the view of adding to the artistic effect of the pile generally, but whether it has rather broken up the outline into too many portions, and so destroyed that unity of idea and that serene beauty which the pure English Gothic invariably creates is a question which will probably suggest itself to some more thoughtful observers.

This appraisal may be seen very much as a contemporary view at a time when the niceties of Gothic Revival architecture were being championed.

Cemetery Chapels, 2012.

Cemetery Chapels from the rear, 2016.

The chapels incorporated gables, dormer windows and three archway entrances. The centre one was intended as a carriage way, the other two for foot passengers. A spirelet rose above. They had octagonal ends and their floors were paved with Minton encaustic tiles.

Though the Bishop of Lichfield, speaking at the consecration of the cemetery, remarked that churchman and dissenter would be alike in death, there had nevertheless been provided a chapel for Episcopalians (Church of England) and one for dissenters. We might compare this circumstance with prevailing views in Burslem, where there were discussions in May 1878 regarding whether or not to build two chapels in the town's own intended municipal cemetery, or whether to erect only one, thus keeping expenditure down. Ultimately, Burslem's chapel was used by all denominations, though was demolished in 2010. The grave plots in both of the cemeteries were, of course, divided into sections relating to religious denomination and social class, telling us much about the aims and ideals of Victorian society.

21. Former Portland Works, Sutherland Road, Longton (1861)

John Aynsley (1823–1907) began to manufacture china in partnership with Thomas Cooper and Samuel Cope in 1854 at a works in Market Street in Longton. In 1861,

Former Portland Works, 2018.

Aynsley and Samuel Bridgwood erected the Portland Works. Intended to impress, its fifteen-bay façade combined Italianate features – note the Venetian window – with a Georgian style. A cartouche inside the pediment embraced the factory's date of construction. It was designed in such a way as to offer good natural light for the workers and a well-ventilated interior. As a leading producer of fine china, bustling industrialist and a civic leader, known affectionately as 'the Grand Old Man of Longton', Aynsley was a community activist whose concern for others underpinned his management of the Portland Works. Giving evidence before the Children's Employment Commission in 1862, he stated:

> We always lock up at 6 p.m. Our workmen always leave off at that hour, nor do we ever, except in very rare cases, work overtime. As far as I am concerned, a law preventing children under 13 or 14 being employed at all after 6 would not be inconvenient. In fact, I think such a law would be very good. I would even have all work after 6 prohibited. But then my pockets are large enough to enable me to employ extra hands when necessary. This would not be the case with those manufacturers whose premises are smaller. I have been a workman and have experienced the evil of working in a badly ventilated room; and in building these works it has been my ambition to have my rooms as convenient and well ventilated as possible for my workpeople.

Former Portland Works, 2018.

Aynsley's was an enlightened view. The conviction that a person's morale and dignity might be raised by his immediate environment was increasingly applied to the design of factories and was also recognised by the architects of the new board schools in the 1870s.

Aynsley became known for its fine bone china, especially breakfast, tea and dessert wares, selling many of its wares to the United States and Canada.

The Portland Works was Grade II listed in 1993.

22. Longton Town Hall, Times Square, Longton (1863)

Longton Town Hall, with its market hall to the rear, was designed in the Italianate style by Burrill. Fashioned from blocks of ashlar, it was built with a thirteen-bay frontage incorporating a central porte cochère. Towering Ionic columns and a handsome pediment also catch the eye. It was extended in 1912–13.

Like all of Stoke's town halls, this one came to be a multipurpose venue. Lectures were given here, with Socialist and feminist activist Annie Besant speaking on secularism in 1875. There were musical concerts performed by such as Longton Borough Prize Band.

Above and below: Town Hall, date unknown.

Pragmatists may see the city's town halls as largely redundant and costly to maintain, raising questions about the council's commitment to the built environment and Potteries heritage. However, local pride dies hard.

In 1985, the Secretary of State for Environment refused to grant listed building status to Longton Town Hall, following the city council's decision to demolish it. The council argued that the cost of carrying out necessary structural repairs would be huge and envisaged instead the construction of a futuristic glass-domed extension to the covered market to the rear. The cost of this project would have been in the region of £1 million, in addition to the estimated £250,000 to demolish the Longton landmark. Demolition seemed imminent, especially when the wooden blocks from the hall's ballroom were taken up and later re-laid in Stoke's Jubilee Hall. Gutting of the interior also began.

However, in March, 1986, the Save the Longton Town Hall action group gained a high court injunction to halt demolition at the eleventh hour. In April, Environment Minister Lord Elton reversed the previous decision, bestowing Grade II-listed status on the building, following reassessment of the earlier recommendation. Finally, on 28 May, the council voted to preserve the building.

Restoration followed and Longton Town Hall reopened in 1992, following a facelift that cost in excess of £4 million. Ironically, the building won first prize in the refurbishment section of the Good Design Awards, organised by Stoke Council in 1994, recognising the work carried out since 1986.

23. Wedgwood Memorial Institute, Queen Street, Burslem (1869)

The establishment of this Grade II*-listed building emerged out of the belief that an efficient school of art and design was needed and the desire to commemorate the great industrialist Josiah Wedgwood (1730–95).

Numerous craftsmen would come to be credited for their involvement with the institute, including John Lockwood Kipling and Robert Edgar. They envisaged a Venetian Gothic style that had been popularised by John Ruskin. Other Venetian Gothic buildings of the same period include the University Museum at Oxford, which was built between 1854 and 1860. It is Italianate, very horizontal and rather colourful, like the institute.

Ruskin's theories also influenced the building of the National Academy of Design in New York, which was built in 1862–63. This was reputedly modelled on the Doge's Palace in Venice, highlighting the interest in Italianate architecture at the time.

The institute was unfinished when it opened in 1869, though it dazzled the people of Burslem.

The twelve signs of the zodiac were all represented, crafted in mosaic by Salviati. Below were panels representing the corresponding months of the year, these being the work of Rowland Morris and William Wright.

Over the entrance is a triangular space – a tympanum – with portrait medallions of three people connected with Wedgwood's projects: these are sculptor John Flaxman, scientist Joseph Priestley and Thomas Bentley (1730–80), his business partner.

The panels illustrating industrial processes of the pottery industry represent Burslem's own terracotta army. They depict the clay as raw material right the way through the finished ceramic production. Designed and drawn by Matthew Elden, they were executed

Above: Wedgwood Institute, 1994.

Below: Smith Child's monogram on the Wedgwood Institute.

by Rowland Morris and his assistants. Many public buildings came to incorporate panels depicting local industry. See the brick mural above the Potteries Museum in Hanley. The panels are literally part of the structure itself, just as much as the brickwork is. They are not decorative panels attached to the structure, and in this way, they have a functional as well as an aesthetic role to play.

Wedgwood's statue above the entrance was unveiled in 1873. There were later extensions to the building, but it is the extravagant frontage that has seduced observers over the years.

24. Hanley Town Hall, Albion Street, Hanley (1869)

The successor to Hanley's town hall of 1845 was not a purpose-built municipal building, but a failed hotel. However, the relatively brief history of the Queen's Hotel tells us much about the rise of Hanley and the aspirations of the town's prominent inhabitants.

It was built by the Hanley Hotel Co. (Ltd) and, considering the ultimate failure of the venture, it is interesting to consider the prescient views of one writer in the *Staffordshire Times* newspaper of November 1867. He observed that 'an undoubtedly magnificent pile' was in the course of construction. Intriguingly, the writer questioned whether or not such a huge hotel would pay its way: 'There are not wanting people who say that it will turn out to be a sort of land "Great Eastern" – altogether too big for the requirements of the place.'

The hotel opened on 31 December 1869 and was designed by Messrs Robert Scrivener & Sons of Hanley with French pavilion roofs. It was built of red brick and incorporated quoins of white brick and dressings of Hollington stone. It had a high pitched roof and

Town Hall, date unknown.

Town Hall, 2012.

dormer windows, thirty-eight bedrooms, and cost over £20,000. It had a luxurious interior as well as a bowling green to the rear, stabling accommodation for twenty-four horses, and lock-up coach houses.

It was built to rival the North Stafford Hotel in Winton Square, Stoke, and aimed to attract commercial gentlemen and families. The hotel fell short of expectations, and the 1871 census lists only two visitors to the hotel.

The Queen's Hotel was purchased by Hanley Town Council for £10,800 in the 1880s. The council's alterations cost thousands of pounds and the conversion was supervised by Joseph Lobley who had been appointed borough surveyor of Hanley in 1871. A court for the quarter sessions was established, the former banquet room was converted into a police court, the commercial room became a council chamber, the smoke room became an office for the town clerk's department, a billiard room became a police office and other alterations were made. In 1888, the Victoria Hall was added to the rear.

25. Former Stoke Library, London Road, Stoke (1878)

Stoke Athenaeum and Literary and Philosophical Institution was formed in 1846 in order 'to diffuse among its members knowledge in general'. It offered a library of nearly 3,000 books, a newsroom and a museum, and was based in the new town hall in Glebe Street.

The former Stoke Library, 1995.

The Public Libraries Act of 1850 was crucial in terms of promoting literacy to a greater number and emerged as part of the Victorian era of self-improvement, though it was not welcomed by all.

Many Conservatives and Establishment figures claimed that 'the more education people get, the more difficult they are to manage'. However, the march of literacy was not to be stymied. Stoke adopted the Free Libraries Act in March 1875, and a site for the public library was given by Colin Minton Campbell, the pottery manufacturer and MP. It overlooked London Road. The foundation stone was laid on 10 December 1877.

The library and its attached museum – the Shakespeare Institute, founded by Robert Garner – were opened on 7 November 1878 by Thomas William Minton. A mosaic depicting Shakespeare appears on the frontage, which also boasts blue- and red-brick decoration and large, circular windows. The porthole-style windows give the building a quirky appearance, which has been noted by several commentators, including Alan Godfrey, who declared that it looked 'for all the world like a majestic signal box'.

Considering the opposition in some quarters to the educational advancement of the lower classes, it is fascinating to note that one subscriber gave funds on the proviso that the new building incorporated a canteen for workpeople.

The library, which was Grade II listed in 1991, was the work of builder John Gallimore and renowned Stoke architect Charles Lynam. The museum stored pottery and porcelain items from the nineteenth and twentieth centuries, many of these from the mighty firms of Minton and Spode.

The former Stoke Library, 2013.

An experiment in 1882 saw the library opening on Sundays, but was dropped after four years on account of the visits of 'noisy and destructive children'. The building is now occupied as the Chiron Centre, a business specialising in meditation and healing.

26. No. 205 Waterloo Road, Cobridge (1880)

The house was built on a plot of land on Henry Meakin's estate, purchased by Enoch Bennett for £200 in 1879 and is famous for being the home of Potteries writer Arnold Bennett (1867–1931) between 1881 and 1889. The 1881 census for this property lists Enoch as the head of the household, a thirty-seven-year-old solicitor. Also listed are wife Sarah and children Enoch Arnold (the later author), Frank, Fannie, Eliza Tertia and Septimus.

As a novelist, Bennett wasted nothing of his own life experiences, and the house is described in *Clayhanger*, through the eyes of young Edwin.

The house was notably occupied as the Arnold Bennett Museum between 1960 to 1978. The late *Sentinel* reporter and avid Bennett fan John Abberley has previously stressed the importance of the house – 'you could say it was the birthplace of the Five Towns novels' – while noting some of the reasons for the museum's demise. Less recognised are the observations of writer Mervyn Jones, who visited in 1961: 'The woman who looked after the place received me with bored politeness. She was paid by the Council, she said … It was evident that she was not at all interested in Arnold Bennett.' Jones describes the relative

No. 205 Waterloo Road, 1994.

No. 205 Waterloo Road, 2018.

paucity of Bennett memorabilia, and a visitors' book: 'Every day, in a fair round hand, the custodian inscribed the date and the number of visitors. On weekdays it was nearly always a full, decisive naught. I went back a month and counted about a hundred schoolchildren, two Frenchmen, three names from Scotland, and five Americans. There was no record of any adult residing in the Potteries.' Jones adds of his sojourn in the Potteries, 'I met no-one who had read his [Bennett's] books.'

The Arnold Bennett Society has been assiduous in promoting the cultural significance of the house, while a bronze statue of Bennett, unveiled in Hanley in 2017, is also playing its part in raising awareness and interest in one of the city's most illustrious sons.

27. Tunstall Town Hall, High Street, Tunstall (1885)

The Town Hall opened on 29 October 1885, replacing an earlier town hall building of 1816 that had stood in Market Square. The architect was A. R. Wood, and the Town Hall displays typical elements of his functional approach to building design.

The Town Hall and Public Offices were built between 1883 and 1885 and were attached to the existing covered market, which was renovated and improved at this time. The Town

Town Hall, 2012.

LAID BY

GEORGE . CUMBERLIDGE . ESQ.

CHIEF BAILIFF.

5TH . DAY . OF . SEPTEMBER . 1883.

A . R . WOOD . ARCHITECT.
J . GROSVENOR . CONTRACTOR

Detail on the Town Hall.

Hall could accommodate 1,100 people and the lighting, both natural and artificial, was described in 1907 as being 'of the best'.

The impressive Renaissance-style façade boasted a nine-bay frontage incorporated a lower storey of rusticated stone. The upper storey, of red brick and stone dressings, included balustraded balconies.

The old clock face at the top of the middle bay of the Town Hall was replaced long ago by what is wrongly assumed to be the Star of David, fashioned in ironwork. It is thought that the weight of the masonry above the clock was beginning to crush what was beneath, and so the iron spars were added to evenly distribute the weight around the circular hole.

The story of this Town Hall differs to others in the Potteries in that it was the intention from the start to incorporate shop premises. From the start, one of the shops in the basement of the building was leased by the Tunstall Coffee House Co., whose premises were offered to the working man as an alternative to the public house. The north end of the front of the building was occupied by the National Provincial Bank.

The Town Hall helped to raise Tunstall's status, even though it was only classed as an urban district at the time of Federation in 1910 – hence the boast of former Chief Bailiff T. G. Booth in 1890: 'They all knew that Tunstall was a very young town, and that the popular name for it was "That robust youth"… They were striving ahead of the mother town of Burslem, and they always wanted to lead the way instead of being left behind.'

28. Victoria Hall, Bagnall Street, Hanley (1888)

The Victoria Hall was envisaged in 1883, when Alderman Hampton expressed that he 'would like to see a hall erected at the back of the Queen's' – which had, in that year, been bought by Hanley Borough Council for intended conversion into a town hall.

The Town Hall Committee aimed to construct a venue capable of holding a larger number of people than anywhere else in the Potteries. The building's foundation stone was laid in 1887, and the hall – which commemorated Queen Victoria's Golden Jubilee – opened in October 1888, swiftly becoming the focal point for music in the Potteries. It was designed by Joseph Lobley, borough surveyor of Hanley, and was added on to the back of the building of 1869 on the site of the hotel's bowling green. The building contractor was T. Godwin.

The building was 64 feet wide by 133 feet long and contained two galleries and a large orchestra. It was envisaged that the hall would seat 2,800 people but that, when necessary, it would be possible to redistribute seats and use corridors so that 5,000 people might be accommodated. The Victoria Hall cost £14,000 becoming the finest concert hall in North Staffordshire.

The Victoria Hall organ was made by Messrs Gonacher & Co. of Huddersfield for the Saltaire Exhibition and was purchased 'at a price much below its real value' for the Victoria Hall. In 1922, the organ was rebuilt by Henry Willis III, an organ builder of considerable renown. He also looked after the organs at Liverpool and Westminster cathedrals.

Victoria Hall, 1994.

Victoria Hall and car park, 1996.

In 1896, Elgar conducted his cantata 'King Olaf' for the first time in the Victoria Hall. In September 1945, Stoke-on-Trent Choral Society staged a victory concert to commemorate the end of the Second World War. The year 1997 saw the Victoria Hall – a listed building – being refurbished to transform it into a venue fit for the twenty-first century. In September 1998, the hoardings were removed from the new glass, tile and steel atrium, which now embraces front of house facilities and bars. This extension was designed by London architects Levitt Burnstein, with advice from English Heritage.

29. Middleport Pottery, Port Street, Middleport (1889)

The design requirements of working factories relating to the efficient movement of workers and materials had been seen in the reconstruction of Messrs Twyford's Cliffe Vale sanitary works in 1887.

Hard on the heels of this factory was a much-praised model pottery erected on the banks of the Trent and Mersey Canal: the Middleport Pottery of Burgess and Leigh, which firm claims the questionable foundation date of 1851. It was the first factory commission undertaken by that versatile and functional architect, Absolom Reade Wood, and could boast of seven bottle ovens.

H. G. Wells' description of Wedgwood's Etruria Works in 1888 (see later entry) should be considered in the light of what was taking shape at Middleport at the same time. The layout of the factory was eminently practical, allowing for the coming and going of men and materials with the least possible fuss. It was built on a quadrangular plan,

Middleport Pottery from Port Street, 2014.

the site extending over nearly 1.5 acres. Parallel lines of buildings enclosed courtyards. Departments were kept separate and had their own access, a tried and tested arrangement on pottery manufactories.

In *Anna of the Five Towns* (1902), Arnold Bennett describes the fictional Providence Works, which is widely believed to be the real life Middleport Pottery. Bennett's depiction recognises the emphasis that A. R. Wood always put on the practical, rather than decorative aspects of buildings:

> The architect of Providence Works knew his business and the business of the potter, and he had designed the works with a view to the strictest economy of labour. The various shops were so arranged that in the course of its metamorphosis the clay travelled naturally in a circle from the slip-house by the canal to the packing-house by the canal: there was no carrying to and fro.

There were good working conditions for employees at Middleport Pottery. It included a wash house for workers with soap fountains and dispensers. Such a facility was crucial, considering the numerous instances of workers' deaths through lead poisoning (lead glazes being widely used in the pottery industry).

The pottery is still trading and incorporates excellent museum, educational and café facilities.

Middleport Pottery from the Trent and Mersey Canal. Drawing by Mervyn Edwards.

3c. Fenton Town Hall, Albert Square, Fenton (1889)

Designed by R. Scrivener & Son of Hanley, this building is described by Pevsner as 'brick, symmetrical, Gothic – but with a number of little originalities which help to relieve the portliness of the building'.

It is almost a cliché to state that our town halls were an expression of municipal pride, but was Fenton – whose local government was the responsibility of a Board of Health by 1873 – keen to develop its own civic identity? A study of the origins of the town hall project provides some answers.

A town/public hall for Fenton had certainly been proposed by 1875, to meet the need to accommodate the growing number of local government services.

In September, numerous ratepayers expressed disapproval of the idea to erect the hall in Church Street (now Christchurch Street). It was, they said, not a suitable site. Church Street was little more than a private street, and the hall needed to be erected in a far more public location. Moreover, 'an amendment in favour of no Town Hall being erected was carried'. The board, however, had already accepted architectural plans and decided to press ahead with the project – especially as the Church Street site was the only one that could be obtained at the time. It was also stated that to build the hall near a main road would risk the meetings therein being disturbed by the noise of cart traffic outside.

Public opinion was much aroused in the local press. *Observer* questioned why the board wanted to spend £10,000 on 'a town hall of some architectural pretensions in a back street'. 'A Rate-payer' clearly saw the Town Hall as a council vanity project. He quibbled

Above: Town Hall, date unknown.

Below: Town Hall, 2014.

over the cost, citing burial accommodation, roads and sewerage as more important than the 'luxury' of a town hall. Other letter-writers suggested alternative sites.

Nothing happened until early 1886, when William Meath Baker offered to build the Town Hall as part of a planned development of new streets and public and private buildings. The Town Hall opened in 1889 and Fenton's Urban District Council, formed in 1894, bought it from Baker in 1897.

31. Christ Church, Christchurch Street, Fenton (1890)

Fenton's original (Anglican) Christ Church was consecrated in 1839, thanks to the munificence of Ralph Bourne of Hilderstone Hall (died 1835).

The Bournes and the Bakers in Fenton – two potting families connected by marriage – were benefactors of Christ Church over the decades. William Meath Baker gave the adjacent Town Hall to Fenton and oversaw the construction of Albert Square, and it is in the context of an industrial family's paternalism that we need to view the history of Christ Church. When the old church became damaged by subsidence, the new Christ Church was built in 1890, with a memorial to William Baker IV (died 1865) being transferred from the old church to the new. The tablet declares that Baker 'built this church, vicarage house, and infant school, gave the organ, and augmented the living'. His memorial can be found in the churchyard.

The church could seat 1,900 people and was designed by Charles Lynam in the Decorated style. It was built from red brick and stone dressings, and its solid west tower of eight bells was added in 1899. Pevsner famously described the church as Lynam's magnum opus – 'magnum, however, only in size'. It was listed Grade II in 1989.

Christ Church, 2005.

Christ Church Tower, 2014.

32. Jubilee Buildings, the Boulevard, Tunstall (1889–91)

The Jubilee Buildings may be regarded as an unwieldy clump of amenities, though notable because no other structure illustrates the functionalism of architect A. R. Wood (1851 – 1922) as well. His *Sentinel* obituary recorded that 'if he paid more attention to the

Jubilee
Buildings
entrance,
1994.

Jubilee Buildings, 2012.

interior convenience of his buildings than to the exterior, it was a saying of his that if the planning were all right, the elevation could look after itself'.

The project was the brainchild of John Nash Peake who, in the mid-1880s, advocated accommodation for students of science and art. It was then decided to erect such a building in order to commemorate the Golden Jubilee of 1887. Wood, the town surveyor, drew up plans for a building, which would be multifunctional.

The foundation stones of the Queen Victoria Jubilee Buildings were laid on 16 May 1889 and the official opening took place in October 1891. The local press reported that they were 'designed more with a view to utility than ornament.' Likewise, they were described by Pevsner in 1974 as 'indifferent'.

The new edifice had a Renaissance-style frontage incorporating red-brick and terracotta dressings.

In October 1895, the foundation stone of new extensions to the Institute were laid. They were opened in 1897, embracing a domestic science school, pottery decorating rooms for the art school, a museum and an art gallery. The Jubilee Buildings embraced many town institutions, including a School of Art. Its rooms were all on the first floor and the large windows faced due north, allowing students ample natural light in which to undertake close work. The French system of seating pupils was used, with each student occupying a moveable desk entirely to himself. This was particularly advantageous when students were drawing an object from life.

The large swimming bath was opened, partly complete, in 1890. The Drill Hall with its adjoining volunteers' armoury was built in Greengates Street in 1898. Other additions were a Town Yard and a depot for the town's steam fire engine and apparatus was provided as well as a mess room for the fire brigade.

The town's free library was removed here in 1891.

33. Former Miners' Hall, Moorland Road, Burslem (1893)

Located in what had been a heavily mined area of Burslem – the 1878 Ordnance Survey map shows the proximity of the Jackfield, Hamil and Bykers (Bycars) collieries, while a Colliers' Arms beerhouse traded in Moorland Road – the Miners' Hall was not only a brick and mortar testament to miners' solidarity but to a more considered form of trade unionism that leaned towards conciliation.

It was erected by the North Staffordshire Miners' Federation, incorporating an agent's residence, committee room, offices and a spacious assembly room. Designed by J. R. Wood, a Waterloo Road architect, it was built by W. Cook, of Burslem.

Enoch Edwards (1852–1912), a Primitive Methodist, trade union leader and MP, commented upon the laying of the foundation stone that miners had long desired a conference hall in which they could discuss their concerns. It is interesting to contemplate how the opening of the miners' hall in 1893 may have been triggered not only by the forming of the Sneyd Colliery Co. in 1875, but by the nature of industrial relations at the time.

Former Miners' Hall, 1996.

Former Miners' Hall, 2018.

Edwards, a towering trade unionist figure who favoured arbitration rather than provocation, remarked that twenty years previously, relations between capital and labour had been strained. However, he continued, employers had since found that trade unionism, properly applied and carefully understood, was not damaging to their interests. Mr G. Leveson-Gower MP hoped that the hall would become 'a temple of harmony and peace'. Though the mining industry was to know much strife and many vicissitudes over the course of the next century, the speeches made when laying the hall's foundation stone make it clear that sundry notables were promoting collective bargaining – at least in principle. Mr James Heath MP stated that 'although he was sorry he could not agree upon one of the most important questions affecting the mining industry, he had never opposed the spread of trades unionism, but, on the other hand, he believed that the stronger they made their unions the better it would be for the miners themselves and the employers of labour'. The struggles in the mining industry over the following century would severely challenge this spirit of entente.

34. Clock Tower, Tower Square, Tunstall (1893)

The plight of the poor in Tunstall did not go unnoticed by some enlightened philanthropists. The present clock tower was erected in memory of a great Tunstall benefactor, Sir Smith

Clock tower, 2010.

Clock tower, 2017.

Child, of whom there is a bronze bust in a niche on the east side. Erected on the former site of the Town Hall/Court House (demolished in the early 1890s), the tower was built of yellow brick and is around 50 feet high. On its north face is a plaque that reads:

THIS TOWER was erected by Public Subscription A.D 1893, in the Town of his birth and in the 86th year of his age, IN HONOUR OF SIR SMITH CHILD, BART. A PHILANTHROPIST, who, foremost in every good work by generous gifts and wise counsel, sought to brighten the lives of the WORKING CLASSES, and by noble Endowment of Convalescent Homes offered a priceless boon to THE SUFFERING POOR.

Sir Smith Child (1808–96) was a Tunstall MP who retired from politics in 1874 at the age of sixty-six. He was created a baronet in 1868. He was a major Potteries philanthropist, contributing to numerous charities.

There is an almost identical clock tower in Barnstaple in Devon, dated 1862, designed by R. D. Gould.

Contemporary press reports of the unveiling of Tunstall's clock tower reveal that it was designed by Edward Webb, architect, and built by Messrs Inskip of Longton. Webb 'had received great assistance from Mr A. R. Wood'.

The clock tower gave Tunstall's market square a focal point and a town landmark with which it has been identified ever since 1893. Tunstall people, often accompanied by a band, formerly gathered around the tower on 31 December in order to see in the New Year.

Necessary repairs projected to cost £52,000 prompted Councillor Barry Stockley to tell *The Sentinel* in 1991: 'With the financial problems [Stoke Council] is facing at present … it would be a complete waste of money to spend £52,000 on this. I would rather let it collapse.' However, it was ultimately cleaned and repaired before being re-unveiled in its centenary year of 1993.

35. Walkers' Nonsuch Ltd premises, Calverley Street, Longton (1894)

A blind person could be taken to this Potteries site and would instantly guess the location. This aromatic toffee factory is to found in Calverley Street, formerly Lovatt Street. Walkers' Nonsuch toffee derived its name from Henry VIII's sumptuous 'Nonsuch' palace, so renowned for its magnificence that there was 'nonsuch' like it.

Company founder Edward Joseph Walker aimed to create toffee that defied comparison with any other, but his enterprise had humble beginnings. He ran a small sweet shop in Stafford Street (now the Strand) in Longton, but began to make toffee at the rear of the premises. Later, Edward recruited his son, Edward Victor, and they manufactured the toffee to Edward's original recipe. With production increasing, it became necessary to open a small factory in King Street to cope with the demand. There are surviving photographs of the company's old delivery vans. An independent company with limited liability emerged in 1922. The firm moved to an old sweet factory, run by boiled sweet makers Horleston Brothers Ltd and built in 1894. Its date stone is clearly visible above the original entrance gate. Walkers' grew through the acquisition of Horleston in 1947 and Siddalls Blue Churn Confectionary in 1961.

Over the years, this family run company has attracted much media interest – perhaps especially in the 1980s when it was suggested that its toffee might have

Above and below: Walkers' Nonsuch factory, 2012.

aphrodisiac properties. When a quarter of the female staff became pregnant at the same time, the story was picked up by the BBC's *That's Life* programme, with presenter Esther Rantzen plying ladies in London with the confectionary to see if it would increase desire.

In 1994, the company sent HRH the Queen Mother a consignment of toffee in order to mark her birthday. In 2017, Ian Walker, the grandson of founder Edward Joseph, died at the age of eighty-one, having worked for the company for sixty-two years. He had served as managing director for thirty years, stepping down only two months before his death. Today, the company makes over 1.25 million toffees a day and sends them to forty-five countries around the world.

36. Former Bratt & Dyke shop, Trinity Street, Hanley (1896)

The erection of this emporium helped to cultivate Hanley's status as the retail capital of the Potteries.

Oliver Dyke, the son of a Cheshire farmer, was born in 1860, serving an apprenticeship in the drapery trade before working in several provincial towns and for a large establishment in London. Arriving in the Potteries 1890, he went into partnership with

Bratt & Dyke store, 1950s.

Former Bratt & Dyke store, 2012.

Henry Bratt, of Northwich. They bought Dudley's mantle business in Stafford Street. The venture was started in defiance of advice that Dyke had received from a business friend: 'Not only was the business proposed to be taken over itself wanting in public confidence, but the town was about the last place on the face of the earth for a pushing man of trade.'

Bratt and Dyke, however, felt that they could prosper, on account of the store's central location and the fast-increasing local population. They began to sell a range of goods, but soon saw the need to expand.

Their purpose-built, three-storey department store was erected in 1896 and opened in 1897 with the premises being known as The Central.

Bratt and Dyke advertised themselves as drapers and milliners, selling dresses, jackets, lace goods, etc. The basement of the new premises was used as a warehouse, and there was a large dining room and kitchens incorporated. It was reported that the store was run by 'a contented family, the principals, heads of departments, and assistants sitting down to the same tables'.

The ladies' department was supervised by Mrs Dyke, and by 1901 the assistants had increased in number from five to thirty. Rooms above were used for the accommodation of those staff who lived on the premises, and who had to obey strict regulations. They were ordered to take a weekly bath, attend a place of worship, and were forbidden to indulge in courting activity during working hours.

The store often advertised itself as 'The House of Satisfaction'. Adjacent property was acquired in the 1920s, while in 1937 the shop began to take on the style of a modern department store, making further alterations. It closed, as Hanley's oldest department store, in 1989.

37. Pavilion, Hanley Park (1896)

The plethora of municipal parks in the Potteries and their renaissance over the past few years underlines the importance of structures such as the pavilion, originally built as the beating heart of Hanley's new civic amenity. Designed by Dan Gibson, it overlooked the terrace and the bandstand, bridge over the Caldon Canal and park's lake, all of which were components in an axial line created by park designer Thomas Mawson. This orderliness would have been intended to instil restraint and discipline in visitors – the late Victorians attempting to impose social control through environment. The pavilion boasted a refreshment room where patrons could purchase cakes, cigarettes, cigars, tea and sweets – but no intoxicating liquors. That said, an early twentieth-century photograph shows visitors milling around the pavilion, and a banner advertisement for Allsopp's Lager draped across the building's frontage. The pavilion's facilities encouraged visitors to spend many hours in the park.

The building was built with a central hall, and at each end, tearooms for ladies and gentlemen, both with cloakroom accommodation. Behind the large hall were kitchens and sculleries, with bedrooms for the tenants above. The pavilion is now undergoing major renovation and will shortly be restored as the conspicuous centrepiece of the park.

Hanley Park Pavilion on the architect's plan.

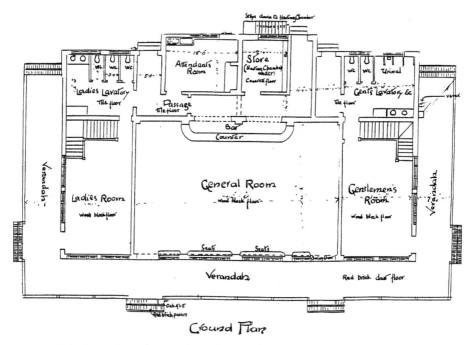

Interior of Hanley Park Pavilion on the architect's plan.

38. Sutherland Institute, Lightwood Road, Longton (1899)

Longton had already established the first municipal park in the Potteries (it is actually in Dresden) in 1888 prior to the opening of the Sutherland Institute on 27 October 1899. It stood on land given by the Duke of Sutherland, who lived at Trentham Hall, and its full name at the time of opening was the Sutherland Institute, Free Library and School of Art. Dubbed Longton's Temple of Learning, the building was designed by Wood and Hutchings of Tunstall and Burslem and boasted three storeys of red-brick facings and terracotta dressings.

It incorporated a reading room and library, art departments and a museum. The relationship between the institute and Longton industry is clearly seen in the establishment of a pottery department as well the School of Art. 'Special attention,' it was stated, 'is given to those subjects having a direct bearing upon the Trades of the District, and it is hoped that Pottery Painters, Paintresses, Engravers, House Painters and others will avail themselves of the instruction given.'

The duke had given money towards the institute's construction and in October 1899 gifted 750 books to the library. The institute was intended to promote an interest in self-improvement through reading and study, though a report in the *Weekly Sentinel* of 9 April 1898 suggests that the Library Committee was not above some small degree of censorship. Thus we catch a glimpse of how new public amenities such as this one were an element in exercising social control. The committee instructed its librarian to black out the betting news in the newspapers supplied to its reading room. This decision had apparently been taken in the interests of those visitors to the reading room who were unable to read the day's news on account of large numbers of betting men poring over the day's sporting tips.

Above: Sutherland Institute, 1994.

Below: Sutherland Institute detail.

The institute, it was believed by some, should not indirectly encourage the racing fraternity. Following much controversy, the decision was ultimately rescinded by a narrow majority.

The institute's terracotta frieze, depicting the pottery and coal mining industries, was added in 1908–09. It was Grade II listed in 1993.

39. Former Falcon Works, Sturgess Street, Stoke (1902–05)

Built by the firm of Goss, and known as the Falcon Works, this derelict factory is a former four-storey pottery works, boasting a stone plaque depicting a falcon on its gable apex.

The company originated in 1858 but by around 1870 was trading at the Falcon Works, Edward Street (now Sturgess Street). Goss erected the surviving workshop and warehouse range as an extension to their original works. The firm, headed by W. H. Goss, was a market leader specialising in heraldic lines, but also producing diverse products such as jewelled scent bottles and vases, brooches and spill-holders. As one of the more prosperous manufacturers, W. H. was in a position to advocate better working conditions for employees and treated his own workers well.

Former Goss Factory, 1995.

Former Goss Factory, 2004.

The Goss family were nothing if not inventive. Nowadays, holidaymakers can buy souvenir fridge magnets carrying the name of the resort in which they have stayed. W. H's son Adolphus conceived the idea of souvenir miniature china ornaments to be sold at holiday resorts. Made of porcelain, they would carry the town's coat of arms and were marketed at the middle and working classes. The items proved immensely popular and were made more collectable by the fact that if you wanted a Land's End crest, you were only able to purchase it in Land's End. The crests, which appeared on such as vases, jars or urns, often copied by antiquarian items displayed in local museums, and were sold by agencies recruited by Goss. By 1900, 481 agencies inland were selling these products. Other pottery manufactories began to sell crested china, proving that imitation is the best form of flattery.

During the First World War, a new industry emerged in the Potteries, with the manufacture of dolls. Heads were made at the Goss factory.

The last member of the Goss family sold out in 1929, later changing hands. The importance of the factory and the ware it produced is emphasised by the existence of a Goss Collectors' Club, while in recent years, campaigner Brian Wilson has battled for the protection of the Grade II-listed derelict building.

40. Golden Cup, Old Town Road, Hanley (*c.* 1912)

If only one public house were to be included in this book, it would have to be the Golden Cup. Though the pub originated as a beerhouse in the later nineteenth century, the date of *c.* 1912 is given here, being that given by the Buckley family (one-time licensees) as the time when the pub's Bass Only ceramic fascia sign was added. In 1964, the pub frontage was altered with the central doorway replaced with a window.

The pub was listed Grade II in 2008, for five main reasons. The dark green faience tiled façade is of high quality, possibly manufactured by the Campbell Tile Co. The Bass Only tiling is believed to be unique. The pub has been altered internally but has retained a good-quality bar counter and back bar, tiling and glasswork. Its façade carries Bass's Red Triangle, the first UK trademark to be registered in 1876. However, the famous triangle had been used on Bass Pale Ale labels from 1855 or even earlier. It was a development of the shipping mark on casks of ale. A bottle of Bass carrying the triangle is even seen in Edouard Manet's 1882 painting, *A Bar at the Folies-Bergere*. The Golden Cup is a striking example of the breweries' aggressive advertising on their tied estates in the early twentieth century. The façade should be compared with that of the Red Lion, which was transferred from Stoke to Crich Tramway Museum in Derbyshire. The Red Lion's ceramic frontage also embraces the name of the brewery – Showell's – and advertises a number of that brewery's products.

Internally, the Golden Cup boasts what is believed to be its original wooden bar with fluted pilasters and a mirrored back bar incorporating drawers. Observe the bell-pushes in the rear right room. They recall the days when patrons could summon a waitress from the more respectable rooms of a public house. Also notable is a glass door pane marked 'Jug and Bottle'. A Jug and Bottle department was a small section of a pub, often accessed from the road outside, where drink could be purchased for consumption off the premises.

Above and below: The Golden Cup Inn, *c.* 1960 and 2011.

41. Lamphouse, former Chatterley Whitfield Colliery, Tunstall (1922)

The Lamphouse was a focal point of the site in the days when Chatterley Whitfield was a busy working colliery and remained so during its museum phase (1979–93). It was built of brick, with four linked parallel ranges and asymmetrical pitched roofs. The miners' self-rescuers, helmets, lamps and lamp-checks were stored in this building. The lamp-checks were a means of monitoring the miners' whereabouts underground. Another feature of the building were the 'Contraband' notices reminding miners that smuggled goods such as matches, lighters and tobacco were not permitted in the mine. Upon the launch of the museum, part of the building became the reception and souvenir shop, but it was here where visiting school parties – upon being equipped with their miner's battery operated cap-lamps and self-rescuers – became the responsibility of the ex-miner guides, who ushered them towards the underground experience. The lamphouse survives in a dilapidated condition but is an important reminder not only of a bygone industry but of a colliery that could claim to be one of the great powerhouses of the Industrial Revolution in North Staffordshire.

The building was given Grade II-listed status on 23 February 1994.

Lamphouse, Chatterley Whitfield Mining Museum, 1992.

Lamphouse, former Chatterley Whitfield Mining Museum, 1994.

42. The Roman Catholic Church of the Sacred Heart, Queen's Avenue, Tunstall (1930)

Architecture, like any art form, provokes diverse opinions. There is, on the one hand, the judgement of the recognised authority, such as Nikolaus Pevsner (1974), who records, a little equivocally, of the Sacred Heart that it is 'large and eager to impress'. A more visceral view was offered by writer Mervyn Jones, who visited Tunstall in the process of writing *Potbank: A Social Enquiry into Life in the Potteries* (1961). He scribed:

> Tunstall, unlike the other towns, is dominated by its Catholic church. It is a huge, ornate, and remarkably hideous building, like one of the latter-day cathedrals in the industrial parts of Belgium and northern France. Some ambitious prelate, one images, must have planned a Counter-Reformation in the stronghold of Primitive Methodism. Along the roof (you look down on it from the park) are five green domes. They have a squashed-in shape and at the centre of each is a kind of stopper of stonework. More than anything else, they look like cylinders devoted to some chemical process. Could this conceivably not be a church after all, but an incense factory? Anything seemed possible.

The church was designed by J. S. Brocklesby, the architect of the Roman Catholic church of St Joseph in Burslem, with the parish priest, Patrick Ryan, as the clerk of the works. It was built of Derbyshire stone in the Byzantine style of the twelfth and thirteenth centuries, with stained-glass windows by the renowned artist Gordon Forsyth.

Roman Catholic Church
of the Sacred Heart, 1991.

Roman Catholic Church of the Sacred Heart, 2018.

Jones' comment that this was a Catholic cathedral erected in a town in which Primitive Methodism originated, invites reflection. The building is a tribute to secular co-operation, being erected through the direct labour of miners, factory workers and labourers. It was a Methodist, George Barber, who as Lord Mayor of Stoke-on-Trent, remarked in 1930 of 'the generosity of the very poorest people' of the town who had helped in the building's construction.

Speaking to the local press in 2007, parish priest Father Patrick H. Farrelly emphasised that he wished to 'preach Jesus not just to Catholics, but to anyone', Father Ryan having recruited non-Catholics in the building of the church.

43. Pithead Baths and Canteen (now derelict), Chatterley Whitfield Colliery, near Tunstall (1938)

Here's another building type that deserves to be recognised in this book, partly on account of its architectural merits and partly as a reminder of a dead industry.

At one time, there were no on-site washing facilities for Whitfield miners. The local men would trudge home at shift's end, caked in pit dirt and sweat, and have a 'stripwash' in front of the fire. In those distant days, Britain lagged behind other European countries in

Pithead Baths and Canteen, former Chatterley Whitfield Mining Museum, 1994.

providing washing facilities for miners. In France and Belgium the provision of miners' baths was compulsory; and in Germany, both provision and use by miners was compulsory.

The former pithead baths and canteen are located in an art deco building whose existence owed much to the social improvements made in the industry in the early twentieth century. A plaque displayed at the time of the building's opening read:

> MINERS WELFARE FUND WHITFIELD COLLIERY PITHEAD BATHS. THESE BATHS ERECTED BY THE MINERS WELFARE COMMITTEE IN PURSUANCE OF THE MINING INDUSTRY ACT OF 1926 WERE OPENED AND HANDED OVER TO THE TRUSTEES ON 29th JANUARY 1938.

This period saw pithead baths/canteen buildings being opened at many other local collieries including Sneyd (1931), Norton (1932), Hanley Deep (1932) and Wolstanton (1940). These buildings were the great social centres at colliery sites, also displaying noticeboards about health and safety or sports and recreation.

Pithead Baths lockers, former Chatterley Whitfield Mining Museum, 1999.

The entrance to the present canteen was previously the 'clean' entrance to the baths. The men would leave their home clothes in the 'clean' lockers, before collecting their pit clothes from the 'dirty' lockers. There were around 3,500 of each in the building. Once they had changed, the miners would exit by the 'dirty door' and proceed to the lamphouse en route to the pit top.

It was noted in 1946 that 'the feeding staff in the new canteen were doing a splendid job, but despite a total of 115,480 meals served during the year, only 20 per cent of employees were using the canteen'. Employees were asked to make more use of the facility, 'especially those under 21, who could have meals at half price'.

44. Wedgwood factory, Barlaston (1940)

In *The Road to Wigan Pier* (1937), George Orwell wrote: 'The typical post-war factory is not a gaunt barrack or an awful chaos of blackness and belching chimneys; it is a glittering

Wedgwood factory, 2016.

Wedgwood statue, outside Wedgwood Museum, 2016.

white structure of concrete, glass and steel, surrounded by green lawns and beds of tulips.' In writing this, he may well have been thinking of the amazing D10 factory opened by the Boot's Company at Beeston, Nottingham. Designed by Sir E. Owen Williams and constructed almost entirely from concrete and glass, it was opened in 1933 and is now a Grade I-listed building.

The Etruria Works of Josiah Wedgwood was opened in 1769, but its layout seemed antiquated to author H. G. Wells, who, in writing a letter to his father in 1888, described the works as 'ramshackle'.

However, it was not until 1936 that the company's directors made the decision to move from subsidence-wracked, polluted Etruria to the green fields of Barlaston. The new factory was built on the Barlaston Hall estate, which comprised 381 acres of open countryside.

It officially opened in 1940, though it remained work in progress for some time. It was intended, like D10, to offer comfortable working conditions for employees at the same time as improving production through a factory layout that would promote maximum efficiency.

One of the inspirations for the new Wedgwood location was Hertfordshire's Welwyn Garden City, initiated by the social reformer Ebenezer Howard in 1919/20. It was the first experimental venture in the Garden City Movement to be designated a new town. One of its planners, Louis de Soissons, created the new housing estate for Wedgwood employees at Barlaston.

Wedgwood's new factory was designed by Keith Murray and C. S. White. It was modernist and used the latest materials and technology. Its internal layout was the responsibility of Tom Wedgwood, an accomplished planner and engineer, and Norman Wilson, the works manager, who emphasised the links between a pleasing working environment and happy and productive staff. The iconic Waterford Wedgwood UK company continues to thrive today on-site.

45. Vale Park, Hamil Road, Burslem (1950)

Vale Park's importance to Burslem – a town that is suffering from neglect and under-investment – cannot be stressed too highly. The club brings revenue into the Mother Town and its stadium offers dining and conference facilities and so can claim to be a social hub.

The club had previously been based at the Old Recreation Ground in Hanley, prior to the opening of Vale Park.

In the mid-1940s, six old pitshafts and a marlhole could be found in the location of the later football ground. Excavation work started in 1944 with earth being moved to create banks for the terraces. In early August of 1950, a crowd of 10,700 inspected the new stadium, which boasted a pitch measuring 123 yards by 35 yards and judged to be one of the best in the country. Vale manager Gordon Hodgson declared that 'if the team could not play on a ground like this, they could not play at all'. The new ground was dubbed 'the Wembley of the North'.

On 24 August, an estimated 30,000 watched Port Vale beat Newport County 1-0, with a 63rd-minute goal by Walter Aveyard. It was reported that some supporters 'swung their hand-bells lustily' in the excitement.

Port Vale vs Shrewsbury, 2013.

46. Mitchell Memorial Youth and Arts Centre (now the Mitchell Arts Centre), Hanley (1957)

Reginald Joseph Mitchell was born in Congleton Road, Butt Lane, in 1895 and died in 1937. He designed the Spitfire fighter plane and is, in the opinion of many, the most important individual ever to have had an association with Stoke-on-Trent. The significance of this building lies in its function as a memorial to Mitchell and also in its role as one of the great cultural landmarks of Stoke-on-Trent.

It was opened in October 1957 by Group Captain Douglas Bader, who had flown Spitfires in the Battle of Britain. The building operated as a youth centre under the control of the city's education service. The venue has, over the years, hosted various activities such as a youth boxing tournament, amateur dramatics and lectures. Run by the Mitchell Memorial Youth Art Centre Trust, it reopened its doors after a major refurbishment in 2011. The new look is very contemporary. Glass-fronted buildings with slantendicular roofs have been in vogue for some time – think of Burslem's old Ceramica Shop as a local example. However, the wing-like curved roof of the theatre's café extension, overlooking Broad Street, is not merely a variation on a current fad, but a thoughtful and deliberate nod to Mitchell's Spitfire design.

The Reginald Mitchell statue unveiling ceremony, 1995.

Mitchell Memorial Theatre, 2012.

47. Potteries Shopping Centre (now Intu Potteries; 1988)

Upon opening, this new retail behemoth was Stoke's answer to other destination shopping malls in the Midlands. The Potteries Shopping Centre was built by Shepherd Construction and the brickwork subsequently won the National Brickwork Award. Stoke's new, multi-floor retail cathedral was functional though charmless aside from the delightful murals depicting local life, executed by talented artist David Light. In June 1989, *The Sentinel* quoted the views of Conservative councillor Ian Parry, who described it as a 'glitzy retail Tardis' that was responsible for the closure of twenty stores on prime city centre sites and the neglect of Hanley's East Precinct.

Compared to other shopping malls, the design of Intu Potteries is safe, unchallenging and unspectacular, in common with many others. Its aesthetic appeal pales into insignificance as compared to the stunning originality of Selfridge's department store in Birmingham or the sumptuous beauty of the rococo/late baroque – and very eclectic – Trafford Centre in Manchester.

Above: Potteries
Shopping Centre, 2012.

Left: Potteries Shopping
Centre, 2013.

However, with the passing of the years, familiarity has bred comfort, and the perceived threat posed to Intu Potteries by planned new retail development has, in some quarters, triggered a public protectiveness with regard to the near-thirty-year-old shopping mall.

48. Civic Centre, Glebe Street, Stoke (1992)

This building is not embraced within Stoke's Conservation Area, though elements of its design were undoubtedly influenced by its proximity. It was necessary to create a modern, functional building that blended in with the neighbouring Town Hall. Period street lamps were collected from all over Stoke-on-Trent, restored, and placed in the forecourt of the Civic Centre. Meanwhile, the postmodernist new building fronted the A500, creating a favourable impression of this part of Stoke to those motorists passing through. All the city

Civic Centre, 2013.

Civic Centre entrance, 2018.

council departments previously based at Unity House in Hanley, were moved to the new offices, so this was an exercise in centralising local government departments in a more cost-effective way.

With the arrival of the new Civic Centre, Stoke Town Hall effectively lost its name and became part of the huge new complex, but there remains excellent access to the older building from the Civic Centre reception area. It was hoped that the new arrangements would end the 'confusion and inconvenience' suffered by rate payers, but the recent erection of new city council buildings in Hanley, as well as an aborted plan to sell off the headquarters in Stoke have served to underline the changing nature of local government policy in respect of whether or not to centralise.

49. Westport Lake Visitor Centre, near Tunstall (2009)

Completed in July 2009, the building was a joint scheme between Stoke-on-Trent City Council and British Waterways (now the Canal and River Trust). Its construction was partly triggered by the increase in waterway activity. The Trent and Mersey Canal passes through Westport only a few yards away, and around 12 miles of its towpath had been widened and resurfaced prior to the opening of the visitor centre.

Above and below: Westport Lake Visitor Centre, 2018.

The centre is built on stilts, which serves two purposes. It creates a wildlife habitat directly beneath the building and gives visitors fine views of Westport lake. Patrons of the cafe may take their food and drink out on to a lakeside balcony/observation deck. It has been an eco-friendly building from the start, with an emphasis on sustainable design. It uses energy-saving devices and the walls are filled with lime-rendered straw so as to provide effective insulation. A sedum mat, made of moss and lichen, coats the roof and is designed to attract insects and butterflies. It also offers insulation. The roof also houses both photovoltaic and solar thermal panels that generate power and hot water. The wood cladding comes from sustainable resources and the walls are made from reclaimed brick, including Staffordshire blue brick. The low-flush toilets use collected rainwater. Walker Simpson, the Manchester architects, were responsible for the design.

Staffordshire Wildlife Trust's education team have worked with the centre to provide interpretative panels on the fauna and flora of the lake. On 9 July 2010, Joan Walley MP opened a new learning centre in the basement, intended as a facility for school groups wishing to develop conservation skills.

The centre, whose materials are sympathetic to its surroundings, went on to win several international awards for its design and energy efficiency. In 2009, it was Sustainable Project of the Year runner-up, and it has been commended by the Royal Institute of British Architects.

It is a state-of-the-art design that fulfils the aim of highlighting the regeneration that has taken place in Stoke. It also excels as a community hub for all those – including birdwatchers, anglers and walkers – who regularly use Westport Lake Water Park.

50. Vodafone Contact Centre, Etruria Valley Business Park (2009)

This landmark office building, constructed by Stoke-on-Trent Regeneration Ltd as a joint project between the city council and Birmingham-based developer St Modwen, incorporates eco-friendly features including 100 per cent recyclable metal cladding and a cantilevered wing-shaped roof that reduces solar gain and cooling loads, also allowing rainwater to be collected for toilet-flushing purposes. As we have seen, this is done at the Westport Lake Visitor Centre, while just over the border in Newcastle-under-Lyme, the design of the magnificent Blue Planet Warehouse in the Chatterley Valley also embraces rainwater harvesting for WCs.

The centre embraces bold shapes and attractive corporate colours and in practical terms is a light and airy modern building, divided into north and south wings.

The relationship between employees and their physical workplace has come under increasing scrutiny in the last few years, cultivating the view among the more enlightened that the design of the working environment should support health, well-being and productivity. This appears to have been considered here.

The building is so angled as to take advantage of sunlight, with overhangs for shading. Inside, there is daylight-controlled lighting. Internally, it incorporated from the beginning 850 workstations as well as a 300-seat café and restaurant. Smaller 'refuelling' points offering food preparation areas were also incorporated. A Quietrevolution axial wind turbine is strategically positioned at the head elevation of

Above and below: Vodafone Centre, 2018.

the scheme. The innovative design was complimented by impressive landscaping, with 7,796 shrubs and trees being planted.

The multimillion pound call centre was highly commended at the Chartered Institute of Architectural Technologists' national awards in 2010, for its technical excellence in construction.

It was designed by the Birmingham office of RPS, architects, which company has pointed out that the building uses 450 tonnes of structural steel – the same weight as a fully laden Boeing 747-400. They add that two 747s would fit in the length of the building and carry the same number of people (1,200 people work here). Alternatively, the firm cite that the building is as long as a T42 naval destroyer.